THE NATIONAL AUDUBON SOCIETY COLLECTION
NATURE SERIES

NORTH AMERICAN
TREES

THE NATIONAL AUDUBON SOCIETY COLLECTION
NATURE SERIES

NORTH AMERICAN
TREES

Text by Barbara Burn

Foreword by Thomas S. Elias, Director,
Rancho Santa Ana Botanic Gardens

Bonanza Books • New York

All of the photographs in this book are from Photo Researchers/National Audubon Society Collection. The name of the individual photographer follows each caption.

Photographers' credits for uncaptioned photographs in the front and back matter of this book are (in order of appearance): Townsend P. Dickinson, Bill Bachman, Robert Dunne, A. W. Ambler, Kent & Donna Dannen, Kent & Donna Dannen, Syd Greenberg, Edmund Appel, Richard Parker, Dr. William M. Harlow, Michael P. Gadomski, Tomas D. W. Friedmann, and Robert C. Hermes.

The National Audubon Society Collection Nature Series
Staff for this book
General Editor: Robin Corey
Photo Researcher: Nancy Golden
Production Editor: Philip Madans
Designer: June Marie Bennett
Production Manager: Laura Torrecilla
Production Supervisor: Cindy Lake

Copyright © 1984 by Crown Publishers, Inc.

This 1984 edition is published by Bonanza Books, distributed by Crown Publishers, Inc., One Park Avenue, New York, New York 10016

Manufactured in Italy

Library of Congress Cataloging in Publication Data

Burn, Barbara.
North American trees.
(The National Audubon Society collection nature series)
Bibliography Includes index.
1. Trees—North America. I. Title. II. Series.
QK481.B9 1984 582.16097 84–3024

ISBN: 0-517-447428

h g f e d c b a

CONTENTS

Foreword by Thomas S. Elias
Director, Rancho Santa Ana Botanic Gardens / 7

Introduction / 11
Trees of the North / 27
Trees of the Western Mountains / 35
Trees of the Pacific / 43
Trees of the Desert / 51
Trees of the Eastern Forest / 57
Trees of the Southeast / 83
State Trees / 91
Suggested Reading / 93
Index of Trees / 95

FOREWORD

Although the North American landscape is dominated by trees, people frequently overlook them. Perhaps this is based on the assumption that they always have been there and always will be. Because they don't have hands and feet and other features similar to humans (nor do they run or roar in the night), trees do not have the same initial fascination as a migrating whale, a Bengal tiger, or a mysterious panda in its remote mountainous habitat. Yet trees can be just as interesting—only in more subtle ways. It is truly remarkable to think that some trees can survive for nearly three thousand years and others can survive the extremely rigorous climatic conditions of a mountaintop year after year without any supplemental protection. Yet others, like the giant saguaro cactus, stand like silent sentinels over the Arizona and Sonoran deserts. Consider how adaptable these plants must be to withstand the searing hot summers and long periods without water. Clearly trees are most im-

portant because of their usefulness to people and the varied roles they play in helping to maintain a stable, healthy natural environment.

A quick examination of just a few different trees can begin to show how much variation there is in the shape of trees, types of bark, manner of leaves, and kinds of flowers and fruits. The bark of a tree is almost like a fingerprint; each type of tree produces its own usually distinct pattern of bark. This ranges from the thin smooth gray bark of beeches to the deeply furrowed type found in some oaks. An extreme in bark thickness is found in the giant sequoias of California where the bark can be one to two feet in thickness.

Leaves come in a great assortment of shapes, sizes, and arrangements. Some of the smallest leaves are tiny scalelike ones as seen on some of the junipers and cedars, while individual leaves on the coconut palm can exceed sixteen feet in length. Look at a maple tree and notice how the leaves are arranged opposite each other. Then compare that to the arrangement found on oaks or beeches. Further differences can be seen by comparing the large compound leaves of walnut and hickory trees with the simple ones on most other woody plants.

Flowers also come in an amazing array. Some, like the blossoms of magnolias, are familiar to most of us, but others, like the flowers of an oak or maple, can be easily overlooked. On the whole, most trees do not have large showy flowers. Despite this, they can be a fascinating study in themselves. A portion of each year's flowers will develop into fruits, and the great diversity of fruit and seed types is beyond the imagination of most of us.

But where do we start if we want to learn about trees? It is easy to become bogged down in lengthy reference and technical manuals with unfamiliar Latin names and botanical jargon. However, Barbara Burn has produced here an excellent introduction to some of the common trees of North America. By grouping them according to geographical regions, readers can learn about individual trees as well as begin to appreciate the great diversity of trees we have. Readers can then graduate to more detailed works. But for now, welcome to the green leafy world of trees!

THOMAS S. ELIAS
Director
Rancho Santa Ana Botanic Garden

Claremont, California
1984

NORTH AMERICAN
TREES

INTRODUCTION

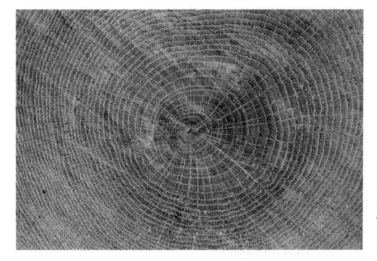

Most of us take trees for granted. We build our houses and furniture with their wood, we read our newspapers printed in paper made from wood pulp, we snack on apples and walnuts grown on trees, and we enjoy the seasonal pleasures of flowering dogwood, brilliant autumn foliage, and Christmas trees. We celebrate trees in our poetry and songs, and we use them to create meaningful images ("great oaks from little acorns grow" and "you can't see the forest for the trees"). But most of us go from one day to the next without consciously thinking about what a marvelous living creation a tree really is. There is much to admire about trees: they are massive, strong, quiet, beautiful, long-lived, and endlessly useful, not just to humans but to many different kinds of animals as well as other plants.

The root system of most trees is vast and complicated, as you can see in this photograph of a dead live oak, which has suffered the effects of beach erosion.
George Whiteley

In fact, naturalists often describe different ecological zones in terms of the trees that exist there, since the presence or absence of trees is what tends to determine the nature of the environment. The treeless regions of the world—arctic or alpine tundra, desert, open prairie—do not receive enough rainfall to support trees and as a result are windswept, arid, and suffer great extremes of heat and cold, affecting every living thing therein. Forests composed of many different types of trees—from the coniferous woods of the north to the tropical rain forests—offer protection from the elements, enrich the earth with organic matter, and effectively control moisture and temperature levels. When a forest is destroyed, either deliberately by humans or accidentally by fire or flood, hundreds of smaller plants and animals lose their habitat as well. The death of a single tree is part of nature's plan, whether it occurs after two hundred years or three thousand (the age reached by the giant sequoias); the decaying wood is eventually absorbed by the earth, and space is created for younger trees to grow. But the death of an entire forest is a catastrophe. It takes so long for the average tree to reach maturity that it might be half a century before a new forest begins to emerge, and even then it would never duplicate the original "virgin" forest. For just as every tree is unique, each forest has its own special character.

It is a simple matter to describe a tree, any tree: a woody plant that grows at least fifteen feet in height and has a single, dominant trunk. (Shrubs, on the other hand, tend to have multiple trunks and are less than fifteen feet high,

though some species occasionally grow to tree size, such as yew and rhododendron.) All trees are anchored in the earth by a set of roots, which also absorb nutrients and water, and they have bark-covered trunks that support a crown of branches, on which leaves grow and fruits develop, containing the seeds that will propagate new trees. This description would work for any one of the more than 750 species of trees in North America, but, of course, there are many differences between trees, individuals as well as species. Most of us can tell a coniferous (cone-bearing) tree from a deciduous tree, which loses its leaves annually. But how many of us know that some coniferous trees are not evergreens and that some deciduous trees keep their leaves all winter? Do you really know the difference between a pine and a fir? Between a beech and a chestnut? This book will show you these differences and many others; it is not designed to be a field guide that will enable you to identify all of the trees on our continent, but it will serve as an introduction to the endlessly fascinating world of trees, featuring some of the most familiar types as well as some unusual and rare ones, all of them native to North America.

Before we look at some of these species, however, let's examine in more detail the basic structure of trees in general and the ways in which these basics vary. All trees have a root system large enough to support and nourish the aboveground growth; the large roots serve to keep the tree firmly in the earth, while smaller roots and roothairs absorb the moisture from which the tree obtains the nutrients it needs. Some species, such as hickories and oaks, have a huge taproot that goes deep into the earth; others, such as maples and willows, have a shallow set of similar-sized roots that grow more or less hortizontally away from the trunk. After a hurricane or windstorm, you may notice that some trees have been upended by the wind and the exposed roots tend to be of the shallow type. Since all tree roots need to obtain oxygen from the earth as well as water, floods can drown a tree, while human structures, such as roads or parking lots, can suffocate it by cutting off the roots' air supply.

The American hornbeam has a thin bark, gray in color, which covers a trunk that is short and often twisted with a muscular, fluted appearance. The wood of this short tree is very dense and hard, giving it the nickname "ironwood."
Pat Lynch

From the roots rises a trunk, which can be tall and straight (as in the American elm) or short and twisted (as in the Monterey pine). The size and shape of most trees are affected by growing conditions as well as by their species; some trees that normally reach a height of a hundred feet in optimum conditions might never grow beyond fifty feet if they are deprived of nutrients or light (such as being shaded by taller, neighboring trees), and shape is often affected by wind and other environmental factors. In addition to supporting the branches, the trunk also acts as a means for nutrients to travel from the roots upward in the form of sap and from the leaves downward to the roots. Most of the trunk is actually composed of dead cells, which we call the wood, the innermost section being the heartwood and the outer sections the sapwood. The only living cells exist just inside the bark; there are three layers there, consisting of the cork cambium, which produces bark; the phloem cells, which transport food from the leaves down to the roots; and another cambium layer that produces new phloem and wood cells. As you can see from a cross-section of trunk, every tree has a series of rings, each one representing a year's growth, which enables us to determine accurately the age of a tree. Some trees are fast-growing, and some are slow; some reach maturity at fifty years, others much later. The black oak, for example, is considered a fast-growing tree; it produces acorns as early as fifteen years of age and seldom lives beyond two hundred years. The Great Basin bristlecone pine is very slow-growing and can live as long as five thousand years, making it the oldest known living tree.

The principal function of bark is a protective one—to keep diseases and insects out and to keep water in. Although all bark tends to be waterproof, each species has a characteristic type of bark, and textures vary enormously from one to the next. Some trees, such as the beeches, have a smooth, thin bark, with a thickness of less than half an inch, while others, such as the sequoias, have deeply furrowed bark that can be as thick as two feet. Birch trees have thin, papery bark that will peel off and that has visible pores; the shagbark hickory, as its name implies, has a rela-

The bark of the paper birch is also very thin and becomes white as the tree matures, peeling readily in large strips that Indians once used to make their canoes.
F. B. Grunzweig

The gingko tree is a conifer, imported to North America from China as an ornamental tree. As you can see, the leaves do not look like those of other conifers, and they are deciduous, but the tree, which may be a very primitive species, produces cones. Hugh Spencer

tively thick bark that breaks into long flat plates, which curl away from the trunk.

The branches are what make up the leafy crown and produce the characteristic shape or silhouette of the mature tree, although this, like the trunk, may be affected by growing conditions. Branches and twigs—or branchlets from which the leaves grow—increase in width each year and also grow in length at the tip. During the winter, when the tree is dormant, a bud forms at the tip of each twig, containing cells that become new growth in the spring and a protective layer of scales that will drop off when the growing season begins. A crucial part of this new growth is the embryonic leaf, which will eventually become the tree's food producer, manufacturing sugars and starches from the water and nutrients supplied by roots and transported by the trunk, together with carbon dioxide from the air and

The bark of many conifers is thick and rough, which in forest fires may help the tree to survive. The bark of this coastal redwood may be more than a foot thick. Kent & Donna Dannen

The eastern hemlock is in the pine family, but its leaves are very different from the longleaf pine (right), growing flat on each side of the branchlets.
Michael P. Gadomski

energy from the sun. Because trees are so large, they need to produce many leaves to keep them going. Deciduous trees generally grow a new set of leaves each year and lose them in the fall; coniferous trees are usually evergreen, retaining their leaves year-round, although each leaf may itself have a life span of only two to five years.

Leaves are probably the most varying aspect of trees, for each species has its own distinct shape. Some are tiny, as in the junipers; some are enormous, as in the palms; some are long and needlelike, as in the pines; some are broad, as in the maples. Some trees grow simple leaves with lobed, toothed, smooth edges; others grow compound leaves composed of three or more leaflets. Leaves can be thick and waxy, thin and delicate, hairy or smooth, and even sharp, as in the spiny mesquite.

Although few people think of trees as flowering plants,

Leaves of the longleaf pine grow in bundles of three at the end of the branchlets; unlike the needles of many other pines, these are exceptionally long—up to eighteen inches—and relatively flexible. Russ Kinne

15

The northern red oak is a typical deciduous tree; its leaves turn from green to brownish-red in fall and are dropped, to be replaced in spring by new leaves. Some oaks, especially those that grow in the south, are evergreen; species in the dry southwest tend to have smaller leaves with less prominent lobes and with a waxy surface to help retain moisture.
Townsend P. Dickinson

each one does produce a flower of some sort, for that is how it produces seeds that will enable the tree to reproduce. Dogwoods and many fruit trees have beautiful, conspicuous flowers, while conifers have only simple reproductive organs that grow inside the cones, but regardless of the type of flower, all trees have these reproductive organs, both male and female, which must be cross-pollinated to produce fertile seed. The male pistil produces the pollen, while the female stamen produces the ovule within the ovary, which will eventually become a fruit containing the seeds. Many tree flowers contain both pistil and stamen; some only have a male or female organ. The pollen reaches the stamen in any number of ways, either carried by wind, insects, or birds; generally speaking (although there are exceptions) the trees pollinated by animals produce showy flowers which attract them, while the wind-pollinated trees, such as the pines, have inconspicuous flowers but produce vast amounts of pollen to ensure fertilization.

Like many palms, the cabbage palmetto has fan-shaped leaves with long blades that radiate from the leafstalk. They are flowering plants, or angiosperms, like all deciduous trees, but the leaves are evergreen like many conifers.
Robert C. Hermes

The shining sumac, a small tree or shrub of the east, has pinnate, compound leaves rather than simple leaves. The sumac is also deciduous, turning a brilliant red-orange in the autumn.
Robert Bornemann

The Rocky Mountain juniper produces cones that are berrylike and attractive to birds. Note how the leaves of this species are scalelike and pressed tightly to the branchlets.   Kent & Donna Dannen

The Douglas fir, a member of the pine family, has a soft cone that hangs downward from the branchlet; both the cone and the seeds provide an important food source for wildlife. Syd Greenberg

Although the Pacific yew is a conifer, producing cones in which the pollen and ovules develop, the fruit is a small red fleshy growth that contains a dark blue seed, which is distributed by birds rather than by the wind, as is the case with pines.
Stephen Collins

Pitch pine cones are hard and woody with spines at the tip of each scale, beneath which the small, winged seeds develop. These cones may remain unopened on a tree for many years, eventually shedding their seeds, which are fed on by wildlife but principally distributed by the wind.
Michael P. Gadomski

19

These are male flowers of the red alder tree, which take the form of catkins; the pollen is spread by the wind to female flowers, which are smaller catkins. The male and female flowers appear on the same tree, but ripen at different times to prevent self-pollination.   L. & D. Klein

This much-enlarged photograph shows the male flower of a sugar maple tree; the petallike lobes are actually sepals, or specialized leaves; the long spikes are pollen-carrying stamens. These flowers grow in clusters at the end of long stalks just below the new leaves in spring, eventually producing seeds with two wings to enable the wind to carry them.   Pat Lynch

Although all hardwood trees are considered flowering plants, this American plum typifies native fruit trees with their fragrant, lovely blossoms, which will produce the seeds in the form of edible fruit. Like many other fruit trees, the plum is pollinated by insects attracted to the flowers and the seeds are distributed by other animals.   Richard Parker

The fruits produced by a tree to contain the fertile seeds take many different forms—flesh-covered (as in apple and bayberry trees) or dry (as in acorn-producing oaks and nut-producing hickories). These trees tend to rely on animals or birds to collect the fruits and spread the seeds, either by consuming them and dropping the seeds or by burying the nuts and forgetting them. Other trees, such as conifers, maples, and elms, produce fruits of varying shapes that can be easily carried by the wind. The seeds contained within these fruits may be tiny or large, but trees tend to produce large numbers of them, for only a few (less than 1 percent in fact) will survive to germinate and become a new plant. Most of them, of course, are important sources of food for wildlife and insects, part of the reason trees are so important to the environment in which they grow.

Flowers of the prickly ash tree, a member of the citrus family, grow in clusters containing many tiny flowers that appear before the leaves. Male and female flowers grow on different trees. The nickname of this species of prickly ash is the toothache tree, because the oil made from the leaves and bark has been used medicinally.
Ken Brate

The clustered female flowers of the red mulberry tree produce sweet, fleshy fruits containing many different tiny seeds.
A. W. Ambler

The fruits, or acorns, of the northern red oak take two seasons to mature; the nut, enclosed in a scaled cup, is an important food for animals and few of the acorns ever survive to become trees, although great quantities are produced every two or three years. Richard Parker

The handsome shiny seeds of the Ohio buckeye develop within a leathery, spined capsule; although this resembles a chestnut, it contains a toxic substance that makes it inedible. Gregory K. Scott

Like other poplars, the eastern cottonwood produces catkins of flowers in the spring, but it gets its name from the cottonlike down that helps to distribute the wind-carried seeds as they are released from the capsule fruits. Vins—CBH

Mesquite trees are members of the legume family, along with peas and beans, and their fruits are pealike pods, containing several seeds, which the Indians used to make food and liquor. Hiram L. Parent

The fruits of the sweetgum tree, native to the southeast, are round and hard with spiny projections; they open in the autumn, releasing their seeds, which are carried by the wind, though the opened fruits often remain on the tree during the winter.   Robert Dunne

The giant saguaro cactus produces showy white flowers and develops a large berry that ripens before the summer rains; the berry breaks open in three parts, revealing the red lining and black seeds, which are quickly eaten by birds and insects. Any seeds that survive will sprout quickly as soon as the rains come.   Jack Ryan

As we will see in this book, trees vary enormously, and this is a function of the ability of trees to survive in different environments and the adaptations they have made in order to do so. Conifers, with their thick bark and leaves, can withstand the cold climates of the north and of mountain habitats, although it is interesting to note that the paper birch, with thin bark and delicate leaves, is also capable of living in the same hostile climate. Birches living in the extreme cold, however, rarely grow as tall as those in moister, lowland areas. Generally speaking, the forests of the North American continent can be classified according to their location, each one with a characteristic group of trees.

We will consider six basic areas in this book, the north,

the mountains of the west, the Pacific coast, the southwestern deserts, the eastern hardwood forests, and the southeast, including the subtropical southern tip of Florida. Regions within these areas may vary considerably, and there may be some overlapping in terms of tree species, but for the most part each of these sections has a special character, the result of climate, geography, and, of course, the types of trees that grow there.

Since many common names are very similar or confusing, the Latin scientific names have been included in the descriptions of our native North American trees. These Latin names are universally recognized and clearly differentiate between trees that otherwise seem similar.

TREES OF THE NORTH

White Spruce
(*Picea glauca*; see page 28.)
Dr. Wm. M. Harlow

The largest continuous forest in the world is a dense coniferous woodland area, also called the taiga or boreal forest, that encircles the earth just below the northern tundra of the Arctic. Stretching from Canada to Russia and northern Japan and China in Asia to northern Europe, this five-billion-acre forest began developing around ten thousand years ago when the glaciers retreated, and for the most part it still exists today, extending southward along mountain ranges and merging with the deciduous woods of the warmer south.

Because of their thick bark and waxy evergreen needles, which are capable of retaining moisture and can continue to function as food-producers even in winter when temperatures rise above freezing, the coniferous trees are ideally suited for the cold climate and snowy conditions of the north. Growing in dense stands, these trees deflect the wind, shrug off the snow with their downsweeping branches, and create a protected environment below on the forest floor, where many animals find shelter throughout the year. Yet there are also some hardy deciduous trees that can survive there, in open areas of the forest where light can penetrate the year-round forest canopy. Birches, aspens, willows, and alders are cold-resistant, tough trees that can be found alongside the pines, spruces, and firs that give the northern forest its evergreen character. In the northernmost part of the forest, trees become stunted in size, and eventually cease to grow altogether; this is the tundra, where the permafrost—a solid, permanently frozen layer of ice that penetrates three feet or more into the earth—prevents tree roots from growing and obtaining water. But where this permafrost does not exist, trees may live, no matter how cold the air may be above ground.

Paper Birch (*Betula papyrifera*; see page 32.)
Bill Bachman

Although coniferous trees appear in other parts of the continent, such as the coastal plains of the east and south, they are so characteristic of the northern forest that it is worth describing this fascinating group of trees in some detail in this chapter.

There are nearly one hundred species of conifers in North America, and all of them share several traits, the most consistent of which is that they bear naked seeds rather than seeds enclosed in fruits or nuts, like the deciduous trees, and these seeds are usually produced in cones, which is what gives the tree group its name. Within the coniferous group, there are four families native to North America, each containing a number of genuses, or closely related species. Within the pine family, you will find a genus of pines, larches, spruces, hemlocks, Douglas firs, and true firs; within the taxodium family are sequoias, giant sequoias, and bald cypresses; the cypress family includes incense cedars, arborvitae, white cedars, cypresses, junipers; and the yew family includes both the yew genus and the torreyas. (To answer a question raised in the introduction, pines and firs each belong to a separate genus but within the pine family; in other words, all firs are pines but not all pines are firs. And to answer another question, the larch is a coniferous tree that is not evergreen but actually sheds its leaves every fall.) Another deciduous conifer found in various parts of North America is the gingko tree, but it is not actually native, having been imported from the Far East and planted widely as an ornamental tree. The gingko is not like other conifers and is believed to be a very ancient plant, perhaps a link between conifers and more primitive plants. Many of the conifers that are seen in the forests of the north are members of the pine family, although many pine species are also common in the south. Pines are classified as either hard or soft, depending on the nature of the wood; many of them are extremely valuable commercially for their lumber, wood pulp, turpentine, tar, and edible seeds.

WHITE SPRUCE (*Picea glauca*)

There are several spruce species in North America, including the widespread Norway spruce, which is not native but

Eastern White Cedar (*Thuja occidentalis*; see page 31.)
Lincoln Nutting

imported. The red spruce is a common tree in mountainous areas of the eastern United States (so-called because its cones are red), but the white and black spruces are most common in the north, throughout Canada and the north-eastern United States. The white spruce is relatively fast-growing and produces cones as early as twenty years of age. It is a tall tree, reaching 150 feet in good growing conditions, with a cone-shaped crown, ideally designed for shedding snow. The seeds are eaten by birds and squirrels, while various mammals, including porcupines and bears, will feed on the bark and the wood directly beneath it. Humans find the tree useful, too; because the wood is soft, it is a major source of wood pulp, from which newsprint and other products are made. A century ago, Americans seemed to believe that their forests were so vast, there would be an endless supply of wood, but we realize now that this natural resource is limited and trees are cut in a system of rotation, enabling new trees to grow to maturity and allowing the forest to replenish itself. The white spruce can often be found growing with other species, such as balsam firs, hemlocks, and birches, but in many areas it is the dominant tree. Its only drawback is an unpleasant skunklike odor, which is produced when its needles are crushed.

BALSAM FIR *(Abies balsamea)*

This tree, because of its attractive fragrance and its handsome shape, is perhaps best known in its role as a Christmas tree, and millions are grown each year for that purpose. When allowed to grow to its full height, the balsam fir can reach ninety feet, though it usually averages between forty and sixty feet. It prefers moist soil and a humid climate and can be found as far south as the Appalachians, though it is most common in central and eastern Canada. Because the bark is thin and resin often collects in pockets beneath, the tree is a frequent victim of forest fires; also, its roots are fairly shallow, which gives it little resistance to strong winds. And it is an important source of wood pulp as well as Christmas trees, so humans account for quite a bit of loss of the balsam fir. Nevertheless, it is fast-growing, especially when it gets sufficient light and moisture, and it remains commercially viable, thanks to replanting programs.

Balsam Fir *(Abies balsamea)*
Pat Lynch

TAMARACK *(Larix laricina)*

This member of the larch family ranges from Newfoundland to Alaska and can be found in relatively low, moist areas, sometimes growing alone in stands and sometimes with other conifers. It rarely grows more than eighty feet in height and its branches are interestingly arranged with the upper ones growing upward, the middle ones horizontal, and the lower ones drooping. The most interesting aspect of this tree, however, is the fact that like other larches, it loses its leaves in the fall after they have turned yellow, although it may hold onto its cones until spring, which gives the tree an eerie midwinter appearance. In spring and summer, however, the tree is lovely, with its yellow cone-flowers and lacy needles, so slender that the sun shines right through them. The bark is rich in tannin and the wood is strong and heavy, but the tree has little commercial value, although many animals, especially chipmunks, squirrels, and mice, rely heavily on the tree as a seed producer.

EASTERN WHITE CEDAR *(Thuja occidentalis)*

The name of this tree can be confusing to some; it is actually a member of the *Arborvitae* genus in the cypress family, rather than the cedar genus, like the Atlantic white cedar native to the East Coast. To make things even more complicated, neither tree is a true cedar, since the *Cedrus* genus is not native to North America at all. Perhaps we should call it by the name arborvitae, a Latin word meaning "tree of life," which was given to the tree by early French settlers who learned from the Indians that it could be used to treat scurvy. Like many other cypresses, its leaves are tiny and scalelike, lying flat against the branchlets on which they grow. It is a slow-growing, long-lived tree that likes a moist habitat and can be found in central and southeastern Canada and in the northeastern United States. Because the wood is resistant to decay, it is often used to make canoes and boats as well as docks and other structures that must be in contact with water. It is not a tall tree, rarely exceeding sixty-five feet, and like many other northern trees it is

Tamarack *(Larix laricina)*
Virginia P. Weinland

cone-shaped on top, although it may not grow branches close to the ground in dense forests.

PAPER BIRCH (Betula papyrifera)

This tree, too, is useful in the production of canoes, for its papery white bark can be stripped and spread over a frame to form an effective shell. (The Indians traditionally used tamarack roots to sew the bark in place.) But the birch has many other uses: its wood is hard and often used for making small objects such as clothespins and toothpicks, and its twigs are important winter food for moose and deer. Together with the aspen, it is a favorite target of beavers. Fortunately, the tree is not in danger of extinction in spite of its value to humans and wildlife, for it is exceptionally hardy, fast-growing, and spreads quickly, thanks to the wind-carried winged seeds that are produced by its catkin flowers. Because of its thin bark it is often the victim of forest fires, but it can regenerate from old roots and will grow well on burned-over land. Presumably because it is so hardy, this tree can tolerate the extreme cold in the north and is found throughout Canada and the northern United States. It can grow as high as eighty feet, but in difficult conditions with a short growing season may reach only forty feet or less. There are several other birches native to North America, not all of them with white bark. In fact, the most common white birches, at least in the east, are not even natives but were imported from Europe as ornamental trees because they are capable of growing in poor soil. These are the European birches and European white birches, which are the kind most often seen in commercial nurseries and garden centers and growing in suburban or urban areas.

QUAKING ASPEN (Populus tremuloides)

Once dismissed by humans as a useless, disease-prone tree, this member of the willow family in the poplar genus is, in fact, one of our most interesting trees. It is perhaps the most widely distributed tree in North America, ranging throughout Canada, the northeastern United States, and south along the western mountain ranges to Mexico. It is neither tall nor long-lived, rarely living as long as two hundred years, but it can grow in many different types of soil and it grows quickly in bare areas, sending out suckers from its roots and sprouting millions of saplings. The value of this ability is immense but in an indirect rather than direct way, for the tree's real usefulness is to other trees and wildlife. It effectively prevents soil erosion in areas where forests have been destroyed, and it provides food for perhaps as many as five hundred species of animals and plants. The quaking aspen is a particular favorite of the beaver and certain browsing animals, such as deer, and many birds depend on its buds and seeds for food. Although its weak wood is not suitable for construction, aspen can be used for various wood products, such as crates and boxes, and is a source for fine magazine paper. Like the paper birch, it likes cold weather and has a thin white bark, but the two species are not easily confused, since the quaking aspen has very distinctive broad leaves on leafstalks so slender that the leaves tremble in the slightest breeze, hence the common name. These leaves turn a golden yellow and remain on the tree after the leaves of other deciduous trees have fallen, lending great beauty and elegance to the autumn landscape.

Quaking Aspen (Populus tremuloides)
Barry Lopez

TREES OF THE WESTERN MOUNTAINS

Engelmann Spruce
(*Picea engelmannii*)
Gale Koschmann Belinky

Between the treeless Great Plains and the belt of land along the Pacific coast is a broad, dry region of mountains, deserts, and valleys that stretches from northern Canada to Mexico. In the western section of this area are the Sierra Nevada and Cascade mountains, and to the east lies the great Rocky Mountain range, which is very grand in scale, with more than forty peaks taller than fourteen thousand feet. This is the most arid part of the North American continent, since the mountains act as barriers for rain-bearing storms that move east from the Pacific Ocean and drop much of their precipitation on the western slopes of the California ranges. As the diminished storms move east, they continue to leave their moisture on the western side of the mountains, creating humid pockets there but desert-dry conditions elsewhere. These slopes and valleys are rich in

tree life, but many parts of the mountain range, including the deserts as well as the alpine peaks, are treeless since there is not enough rainfall to support tree growth. Between the tundralike mountaintops and the deserts and prairies below lie several zones of vegetation, each with its own characteristic species of trees, most of them coniferous. The subalpine zone, which runs from about nine thousand to eleven thousand feet above sea level, contains relatively small trees, while the montane zone (between eight thousand and nine thousand feet) and the foothills zone (five thousand to eight thousand feet) feature larger trees and a wider diversity of species.

ENGELMANN SPRUCE *(Picea engelmannii)*

These handsome trees are closely related to the white and black spruces, but their range is more limited, as they are

Giant Sequoia (*Sequoiadendron giganteum*; see page 40.)
Harold W. Hoffman

Ponderosa Pine
(*Pinus ponderosa*)
Russ Kinne

Rocky Mountain Juniper
(*Juniperus scopulorum*; see page 40.)
Robert J. Ashworth

found mostly in the Rockies at relatively high elevations. They are very hardy trees and grow nearly to the treeline, though they tend to grow taller—up to one hundred feet or more—farther down the slopes where the soil is richer and deeper. Like other spruces, the seeds of this tree provide an important food source for wildlife, and while the lumber is useful to man, it is not important commercially because it inhabits such inaccessible locations, the subalpine and montane zones of the Rocky Mountains.

PONDEROSA PINE *(Pinus ponderosa)*

This is undoubtedly the most dominant tree in the west and is found in abundance on all the western mountains; it can grow at elevations of ten thousand feet or more but does best at lower levels where it can achieve a height of two hundred feet or more and live to be four to five hundred years old. The older trees lack branches on the lower half of the trunk, which is straight, making this one of our most important timber trees. Younger trees have a nearly black bark, which explains the nickname "blackjack pine," while older trees have a reddish-yellow bark, giving the species its

other nickname, "western yellow pine." The name ponderosa comes from explorer David Douglas, who saw it along the Spokane River in Washington in 1826 and thought it "ponderous." Many different animals—from deer and porcupines to squirrels and birds—use the tree for food, either eating the young trees or taking the seeds. The cones, which are about five inches long, turn down as they ripen, releasing winged seeds that can be carried by the wind for several hundred feet.

PINYON PINE *(Pinus edulis)*

This is a common pine of the mountain foothills and mesas of the southwest, a small (up to fifty feet) and extremely hardy tree that can tolerate drought and dry soil. Like many dry-land trees, it grows very slowly and can live for many hundreds of years. It was first named by the early Spanish explorers who quickly learned of the tree's value from the Navajo Indians for whom the tree's seeds (or nuts) were a staple diet. Even today pine nuts are harvested commercially, for they are considered a delicacy, being rather sweet and rich in oil. Every three or four years, a tree will produce

Jeffrey Pine
(*Pinus jeffreyi*; see page 40.)
Kent & Donna Dannen

an exceptionally large crop, so that as many as nine bushels may be gathered from the cones of a single tree. Many birds and such mammals as squirrels, deer, bear, and porcupines feed on the seeds as well, so the tree is considered very important to wildlife. Because the tree can manage to survive even in rocky areas, it often grows in a rather scrubby form.

ROCKY MOUNTAIN JUNIPER
(Juniperus scopulorum)

This small tree is often found growing along with pinyons and ponderosa pines, although it also grows in pure stands with other trees of the same species. It ranges throughout the Rockies, from southwestern Canada as far south as Arizona and New Mexico, clinging to ridges, cliffs, and rocky slopes. It grows slowly and sometimes is considered a large shrub rather than a tree. Like the related arborvitae, its leaves are scalelike, growing pressed against the branches. Male and female flowers grow on different trees, and the mature fruits are small, berrylike cones, which many birds like to eat. In the north, the juniper may grow close to sea level, but in the south can be found at nearly ten thousand feet.

JEFFREY PINE (Pinus jeffreyi)

This tall pine is a close relative of the ponderosa, but is found only in California and Nevada, usually in the montane zone, along with the red fir, the ponderosa, and sugar pines, although it grows in pure stands at lower elevations. The tree is useful to both animals and man, much as the ponderosa is; in fact, the two trees often interbreed, forming hybrid trees in some areas. The needles last for many years, and the branches give off a pleasant aroma when crushed.

GIANT SEQUOIA (Sequoiadendron giganteum)

On the western slopes of the Sierra Nevada in California live the largest trees on the North American continent, some of them over 250 feet in height and 30 feet in diameter. (The General Sherman tree is the largest living example, measuring 295 feet with a diameter of about 110 feet.)

These trees tend to grow in stands together and they appear to be able to resist most diseases and fire, thanks in part to their exceptionally thick bark. Although they grow quickly when young, the rate of growth slows down as they mature and they live a long time, perhaps as long as three thousand years. Although these giant trees are occasionally victims of lightning, man probably has been their greatest enemy, as many trees were cut down for lumber during the nineteenth century. Now, however, they are protected and many of the areas in which they grow have been designated national parkland. The coastal redwoods, which grow on the Pacific coast along rivers or in moist areas, are taller than the giant sequoias (reaching heights of over three hundred feet), but they are not as massive or heavy and do not live as long (only two thousand years!). These two species, members of the taxodium family along with the bald cypress, are survivors of a very ancient American race of trees that once grew as far north as the Arctic.

Pinyon Pine (Pinus edulis)
Dr. Wm. M. Harlow

TREES OF THE PACIFIC

Black Cottonwood
(*Populus trichocarpa*; see page 44.)
Barry Lopez

The mild climate of the Pacific coastal region is caused by the flow of warm oceanic winds. In the north, these winds are accompanied by a great deal of moisture, which in the form of fog, rain, and snow brings as much as one hundred inches annually to certain sections, while the southern part of the coast receives much less precipitation. The land itself is also varied, with flat areas, rolling hills, and mountain slopes, each supporting a different type of vegetation. In the north, the rich forest consists principally of coniferous trees, with spruces and redwoods on the coast and Douglas fir, hemlock, and firs predominating as the elevation increases. In the south, in what is called the chaparral region, few plants reach tree size, but as the hills become taller inland, oaks and pines become the dominant trees. Along the coastal mountains, however, pines and cypresses grow

Douglas Fir (*Pseudotsuga menziesii*)
Russ Kinne

on the western slopes facing the sea, many of them twisted and dwarfed in size by the prevailing dry winds.

DOUGLAS FIR (*Pseudotsuga menziesii*)

Although this tree could have appeared in the last chapter, since it abounds throughout the Rockies, it is one of the most important trees of the Pacific coastal coniferous forest, growing at sea level along the coast but at much higher elevations in the mountains. It achieves its best growth in the lowlands, where it receives a great deal of moisture and can reach heights of over three hundred feet with a diameter of more than ten. Slow-growing at first, and increasing its rate as it matures, the Douglas fir begins producing cones as seeds at ten years but does not reach its most productive period until it is between two hundred and three hundred years old; some trees have been estimated at one thousand

Red Alder
(*Alnus rubra*)
Pat & Tom Leeson

years or more in age. The tree's winged seeds spread very widely and this is often the first tree to grow in ground where fire has swept through, killing existing trees. Wildlife is dependent on this tree for its seeds, and humans have found it a valuable timber tree, using its soft light wood to make large beams, railroad ties, and bridges. The Douglas fir is named for David Douglas, who also named the ponderosa; its scientific name means pseudo-hemlock, for it resembles the hemlock, though it also bears a resemblance to yews (in the leaves), spruces, and firs. Thus, it has a genus all to itself, shared only with the big-cone Douglas fir, which grows in southern California.

BLACK COTTONWOOD *(Populus trichocarpa)*

Although conifers are dominant in the northern Pacific coastal forest, a number of hardwood deciduous trees can be found there as well, among them this impressive member of the willow family, a relative of the aspens and poplars. It can grow at elevations of up to nine thousand feet, but does best in rich, moist lowland soil, especially in the Puget Sound area. It can reach a height of 150 feet or more and grows rapidly, producing flowers and seeds within ten years. The flowers appear before the leaves, in April or May, in the form of catkins, six-inch spikes containing many tiny petalless male or female flowers. The name cottonwood comes from the fact that the tiny seeds are attached to white fluffy down, which enables them to travel for some distance in the wind. The wood is very light and porous and is used in making wood pulp, crating, and excelsior rather than as lumber.

RED ALDER *(Alnus rubra)*

Another deciduous tree of the Pacific northwest, often seen in company with the Douglas fir and cottonwood, is this member of the birch family. Like those trees, it prefers moist bottomland, but it is rarely found at higher elevations. It grows rapidly and like the Douglas fir is quick to seed a forest destroyed by lumbering or fire. Although it is a valuable timber tree because of its straight trunk, it is primarily useful for its benefits to the environment—not for

Coastal Redwood
(*Sequoia sempervirens;* see page 46.)
Farrell Grehan

Interior Live Oak
(*Quercus wislizenii*)
Earl Scott

its food value but for its role as a soil conserver and fertilizer and as a protector to young trees, which the alder will shade until they eventually replace it, since it usually lives less than a hundred years. The flowers are catkins, and the seeds are winged, like the cottonwood, though the alder seeds are contained in a fruit that is a small, woody cone, much like a conifer's.

COASTAL REDWOOD (*Sequoia sempervirens*)

It is believed that redwoods once covered much of the continent before the coming of the glaciers and that these trees and the giant sequoias of the Sierra Nevada, are the only living survivors. These are the world's tallest trees, with the largest living redwood having been measured at over 360 feet. They prefer the humid conditions of the Pacific coast where fog is prevalent, and deep soil, which enables their enormous roots to grow. The wood is of exceptionally high quality, knot-free and durable, and each tree yields a great deal of timber; it was once felt that the trees would become extinct because of overcutting, but many redwoods have been saved, thanks to the creation of national parks.

INTERIOR LIVE OAK (*Quercus wislizenii*)

This interesting-looking oak should not be confused with the live oaks of the southeast, for it grows only on the Pacific coast, along with the very similar coast live oak. These are relatively short trees, rarely exceeding sixty-five feet in height, and their crowns are dome-shaped and broad, presenting a remarkable appearance in the valleys and foothills of California's dry southern coast. Its unusual shape makes it of little value to man, except as a source of fuel. Although this is a deciduous tree, losing its leaves every year, it retains them through the winter and they never lose their green color. These trees grow on rolling hills and lower mountain slopes as well as in valleys and in desert areas, where they remain short and scraggly looking. Trees in this area do not grow densely as they do in the humid north but create an open woodland.

White Fir (*Abies concolor*; see page 48.)
Tom McHugh

46

Monterey Pine
(Pinus radiata)
Maurice R. Castagne

WHITE FIR *(Abies concolor)*

Although this tree can be found in the Rocky Mountains and in northern California, it also grows in southern California, not along the coast but farther inland at elevations of three thousand to eight thousand feet or more. It does best in moist areas with considerble precipitation, which it gets on the western mountain slopes, but it can grow in many different types of soil and is thus a suitable tree for cultivation in other parts of the country, including the east where it is a popular ornamental. The wood is an important source of pulp, though it is also used as lumber; animals,

too, find it valuable for food, feeding on its leaves, buds, bark, and seeds.

MONTEREY PINE *(Pinus radiata)*

Another popular ornamental tree that has been planted all over the world, even as far away as New Zealand, Australia, and Africa, is this small pine of the California coast. Actually, its native habitat is quite restricted—to only three inland locations and three islands, Santa Cruz, Santa Rosa, and Guadalupe. Although the tree will grow tall and

Monterey Cypress
(*Cupressus macrocarpa*)
Noble Proctor

straight in good soil, making it a valuable timber tree, it often remains small and gnarled when the soil is poor and the winds strong and steady. The cones on this tree usually grow larger on one side of the tree and can remain closed for many years, eventually dropping and releasing their seeds.

MONTEREY CYPRESS *(Cupressus macrocarpa)*

This is the picturesque tree of the Monterey peninsula in California, which is the only place in the world it grows

naturally. Because of its contorted appearance, it is of little value commercially, and even local wildlife finds little to feed on. But people cultivate it as an ornamental tree, and photographers and artists from all over the world come to picture it against the rough coastline landscape. Like many other cypresses, its leaves are small and lie like scales against the branches; the cones are small and round. All six species in the cypress genus native to North America can be found in the west, five of them in California where their drought-resistant nature and ability to grow in relatively poor soil enable them to thrive.

TREES OF THE DESERT

Saguaro Cactus
(*Cereus giganteus*)
J. H. Robinson

Because the mountains of western North America pose such a formidable barrier to storms and force moisture-laden air to rise, cool, and drop its water as rainfall on the high ground, extremely arid regions are created to the east of them. These are our natural deserts, which receive very little rain each year, about twelve inches or less, not nearly enough to support a healthy forest of trees. Certain wild-flowers and low-growing shrubs can survive there, but only the hardiest plants can reach tree size, and even these have to develop certain means of storing or conserving water to do so. Depending on its location and elevation, a desert may be classified as cool or warm. Cool deserts, such as the Great Basin, receive slightly more rainfall and suffer greater extremes of temperature—blistering sunlight during the day and below-freezing temperatures at night. These deserts

Mesquite (*Prosopis velutina*; see page 54.)
J. R. Simon

have few trees, although a number of them, including pines and junipers, may grow at higher elevations. Warm deserts, which are in the southwestern states, are even drier and have fewer trees, although the ones that do exist there are among the most fascinating plants in the world.

SAGUARO CACTUS (*Cereus giganteus*)

Succulent cactus plants are among the most familiar desert inhabitants. They take many different forms, from tiny low-growing plants to tree-size growths like this giant saguaro, and many of them develop beautiful blossoms and delicious fruits. The reason that cacti manage to do so well in the dry desert is that they are capable of storing water in their stems and have no leaves through which moisture might be lost. The process of photosynthesis—trapping the sun's energy in order to manufacture food—is carried out in

Joshua Tree
(*Yucca brevifolia*; see page 54.)
K. H. Switak

the stem, rather than by the leaves as in other plants; the cactus leaves have been reduced to spines, which not only shade the stem against the hot sun but also serve to keep animals from eating the stem and fruit. The giant saguaro can grow as high as fifty feet and weigh as much as ten tons, most of which is actually stored water. At first the plant is slow-growing, reaching the height of only three feet in the first thirty years; but eventually the rate accelerates as the branches form. Some saguaros can live longer than two hundred years and their striking candelabra shapes make a dramatic desert landscape, especially where they grow in large forests, as in the Saguaro National Monument in Arizona. The tree does not have a real bark but a leathery covering with vertical ridges that is home to several types of insects, which provide food for birds. Other birds feed on the seeds and the red fruits, making this an important source for wildlife.

MESQUITE *(Prosopis velutina)*

This desert tree is also important to wildlife; the flowers attract bees, which pollinate the plant, while various mammals, including humans as well as deer, rodents, and peccaries, will feed on the leaves and fruit pods. These pods resemble beans, which is not surprising since the mesquite is a member of the legume family, which also includes peas, alfalfa, peanuts, and other valuable food plants. Like acacias, to which they are related, mesquites can survive in the arid desert, preferring old river beds where their deep-probing root systems can tap underground water. They produce leaves and flowers in the spring, losing them during the drought to conserve moisture. The mesquite is a small tree, rarely exceeding thirty feet in height and sometimes remaining at shrub level; the wood is very hard and makes excellent fuel. Like the cactus, the mesquite has spines on its branches, which helps to keep animals from eating a large number of its leaves—to the point where the tree's life is endangered.

JOSHUA TREE *(Yucca brevifolia)*

As its scientific name implies, this tree is a member of the yucca genus of the lily family, and like other yuccas is espe-

cially adapted to survive in a warm desert climate, having the ability to store water as a succulent plant. Some of these trees live as long as a thousand years. Its leaves are evergreen, remaining on the tree for several years; they are shaped like bayonets and have sharp teeth along the edges, presumably to discourage animal browsers. This is a slow-growing plant that does not branch out until it has produced its first crop of flowers. The flowers appear in April or May, and they bloom erratically, sometimes in great profusion. Each "flower" is actually a cluster of hundreds of tiny flowers. The plant is pollinated by the yucca moth, with which it has developed an interesting symbiotic relationship. The moth lays her eggs in the flower itself and the hatched larvae feed on the pollen as they grow; obviously they do not eat enough to endanger the plant's chances for survival, while in the meantime the adult moth spreads pollen to other trees to keep the species going. The Joshua tree, which grows widely in the Mohave Desert, is also of use to other animals, primarily as a nesting site for wrens and owls who use the holes made by insect-eating woodpeckers in the trunk or branches. Humans, too, have found the tree of value, not just for shade and firewood but also for the construction of furniture. The tree is said to have been discovered by the Mormons, who named it after Moses' successor as leader of the Israelites.

CALIFORNIA WASHINGTONIA *(Washingtonia filifera)*

Most people think of palm trees as tropical plants, and many of them are; this palm—named in honor of George Washington—is the only native palm in the southwest, where it can be found growing wild close to the deserts of Arizona and California or as a cultivated tree in cities of the southwest and even in Florida. It is not nearly as majestic as the royal palms, reaching a height of perhaps fifty feet, but it has the distinctive straight unbranched trunk and fan-shaped leaves. The leafstalks are long—up to five feet—and have sharp hooked spines; the flowers grow in clusters and eventually produce berrylike fruits that are nearly black when ripe. Indians used to grind these berries to make flour and used the leaves for shelter, just as many birds still do.

California Washingtonia
(*Washingtonia filifera*)
Charles R. Belinky

TREES OF THE EASTERN FOREST

American Sycamore
(*Platanus occidentalis*; see page 66.)
Dr. Wm. M. Harlow

Millions of years ago, before the Ice Age, the temperate zone of the northern hemisphere was covered with a vast belt of deciduous forest; the climate was milder then and conducive to the development of many types of flowering plants, the ancestors of our trees, shrubs, and flowers today. As the glaciers receded, some ten thousand years ago, they broke up this continuous forest, which has, in more recent times, been largely destroyed by humans, either for lumbering or by the creation of agricultural lands and living space. Nevertheless, there are still pockets of relatively pure forest—and in North America, this can be found in the Appalachians, where more than one thousand species of flowering plants grow.

Although coniferous trees grow among the deciduous ones, mostly in the north and in coastal areas and on mountains, the great majority of trees in the eastern half of the continent are hardwoods that lose their leaves each autumn and grow new leaves in the spring. This adaptation is in response to the freezing climate in winter, which is similar to a drought in that water is unavailable to the trees. Since the leaves of hardwood trees give off large amounts of water, unlike the small, waxy leaves of coniferous trees, the loss of moisture is thus prevented and the growing process slowed down. These leaves, as well as fallen fruit, seeds, and branches, decompose more quickly than the coniferous leaves, creating a rich soil that gives life to many other kinds of plants. When the trees are in full leaf in the summer, the canopy of leaves shades the forest floor, but in early spring and in the occasional gaps that form when the trees are widely spaced, shrubs, wildflowers, and young trees can flower and produce the seeds that enable them to

Sugar Maple (*Acer saccharum*; see page 59.)
Gary Meiter

57

survive. Shade-loving plants, such as mosses, ferns, and fungi of various kinds, further enrich the forest habitat, which is home to an assortment of animals who find food and shelter there.

Within the eastern deciduous forest, variations in climate and topography have resulted in the dominance of certain types of trees. The northern woods are often characterized by maples and beeches, with a number of coniferous species—pines and hemlocks—mixed in. These forests are denser than those where oaks and hickories predominate, since those trees tend to grow more widely spaced, thus allowing a thicker growth at the shrub layer where small trees and bushes obtain sufficient light. Because there is such a rich variety of trees in the eastern part of the continent, this chapter will be longer than the rest, although in fact the present-day forest is only a shadow of what existed even as recently as two centuries ago. Nevertheless, there is still a great diversity of trees, which is, interestingly, not unlike the deciduous woodlands of areas in China, Japan, and Korea; the actual species may differ but the types of trees in the oriental forests are much like those of the eastern United States, due to the fact that they were once part of the same tree belt so many millennia ago.

SUGAR MAPLE (Acer saccharum)

There are many species in the maple family, most of them native to China; several maples are found in western North America, but the most widely distributed American species grow in the east, including the red maple, the silver maple, and, the most familiar of all, the sugar maple. Found from Nova Scotia to as far south as Georgia, this attractive tree, which may grow as tall as 100 feet and live for 250 years, is usually identified with New England, where its sap provides the basis for the important maple syrup industry and where its brilliantly colored autumn foliage is a tourist attraction. The hard, durable wood is used for furniture, musical instruments, and other fine objects, and the tree is valuable to wildlife as well, providing food for deer, birds, and small mammals. Sugar maple flowers are small and hang on

American Beech (Fagus grandifolia; see page 60.)
Townsend P. Dickinson

slender stalks, eventually producing fruits that have two distinctive "wings," which enable them to be carried some distance by the wind.

AMERICAN BEECH *(Fagus grandifolia)*

The beech family of trees is large, including chestnuts and oaks, but there is only one beech species native to North America. (The European beech, of which the copper beech is a cultivated variety, was imported as a timber tree but is now grown mostly for ornamental reasons.) The American beech is often found growing with sugar maples and other species and is distributed throughout the east, reaching its greatest size (about one hundred feet) in the rich soil of the Ohio and Mississippi valleys and on the western slopes of the Appalachians. Although the wood is hard, it does not split or last as well as the maple and is less important as a timber tree, though it is used for making barrels and clothespins. The seeds, or beechnuts, develop inside burrs that ripen in the fall and are a valuable food source for many animals. The bark is thin and smooth, making the tree a victim of forest fires and an irresistible surface for humans who have carved words or symbols on the tree for centuries. It is a beautiful tree that may live as long as three to four hundred years.

AMERICAN CHESTNUT *(Castanea dendata)*

This, too, was once a beautiful tree, widespread throughout the eastern half of the continent. Growing one hundred feet high with lovely spreading branches, it was an important source of lumber and nuts. Tragically, because of a blight that was accidentally introduced into the country in the early twentieth century killing every living tree, the American chestnut has virtually disappeared from the landscape. Young trees will grow, sprouting from the stumps of old trees, but usually reach a height of only thirty feet or so when the blight affects them, often before they have produced flowers or fruit. Much research has been done to restore this tree to its former grandeur, but to date no preventive method or cure has been found. The horsechestnut, which is relatively common over the same range, and also produces white blossoms and dark brown nuts within spiny burrs, is not related to the chestnut but belongs to a different family altogether; in fact, it is not even a native

American Chestnut *(Castanea dendata)*
Charles R. Belinky

tree but was originally introduced from Europe.

AMERICAN ELM (*Ulmus americana*)

This is another beautiful, important species that has fallen victim to a fungal blight called Dutch elm disease, which was first discovered in 1930 and has since killed hundreds of thousands of trees. The American elm once ranged from southern Canada to Florida, growing as high as 130 feet in good soil, with its characteristic fountainlike crown that at one time formed gothic arches over city streets. Efforts are being made to develop disease-resistant strains, but it will be many years before the elm will reestablish itself. A useful tree for its lumber and its seeds, which are important to birds and small mammals, the American elm is perhaps best known for its historical role as a symbol of public life in America. Indians used it as a council tree, and many treaties with the early settlers were made beneath its branches. It was once an important shade tree for village greens and courthouses, where now the depressing appearance of dying trees or the stumps of cut trees is a more common sight. The slippery elm (*Ulmus rubra*) can often be found growing in association with the American elm; it is not as valuable for its lumber nor are its seeds as important to wildlife, but it is a handsome tree, occasionally reaching one hundred feet in height and having a spreading crown rather than the tall profile of the American elm.

AMERICAN HOP HORNBEAM (*Ostrya virginiana*)

Hop hornbeams form a small group in the birch family, and the trees themselves are small, rarely exceeding fifty feet. They are considered "understory" trees, like sumac and alder, since they do not reach the height of the elms, beeches, maples, and hickories with which they grow. They grow throughout the east, often on ridges and slopes, and are probably less well known than their companions

because of their limited value to humans. The wood is exceptionally hard, often called ironwood, but because the tree is so small, it has little commercial importance. The name hop hornbeam is derived from the fact that the distinctive fruit, clusters of flat sacs, resemble hops, and they are closely related to the hornbeam genus of trees, including the American hornbeam, the only native species, which is also known as ironwood.

American Elm (*Ulmus americana*)
Vins—CBH

WHITE OAK *(Quercus alba)*

There are many different species of oak, some of them evergreen and some deciduous, some growing in dry desert canyons and some in low coastal plains and swamps. Most oaks grow in hillside forests, including the white oak, one of our most important and widespread species. It is an adaptable tree, growing well in different types of soil, but does best in rich, well-drained earth, into which it grows a deep taproot. It is a tall tree, up to 120 feet, and because its wood is hard and close-grained, it is a valuable timber tree for construction and furniture. There are two major groups of oaks—white and red—termed originally by lumbermen but now accepted by scientists as well. Both types of oaks

American Hop Hornbeam
(*Ostrya virginiana;* see page 61.)
Vins—CBH

White Oak
(*Quercus alba*)
Townsend P. Dickinson

can be found in the same forests, although the white oak is commonly found with hickories, the American beech, white ash, and other species. The acorns of oak trees are an extremely important source of food for wildlife, and populations of deer, squirrels, and other animals are often affected by the quantity of acorns produced in a given year. The white oak produces acorns every year, with heavy crops every three or four years, while the black oak group takes two years to produce a crop.

WHITE ASH (*Fraxinus americana*)

This valuable timber tree—the wood of which our ax handles and baseball bats are made—is a member of the olive family, a relative of the gardenia, forsythia, and, of course, olive species. Its wood is tough yet lightweight and handsome enough for use as a veneer and paneling material. Its seeds, which are winged, are valuable to many kinds of birds. Ash leaves are compound rather than simple, like those of the oak or maple, with about seven leaflets on each

stalk. Foliage is thickest on the outside part of the rounded crown of leaves, so that one can stand at the foot of the straight trunk and see clearly to the top, an advantage for birdwatchers. The ash grows to an average height of eighty feet, and new saplings grow from the roots of fallen trees. Found throughout the east, usually with beeches, willows, oaks, and hickories, the white ash prefers rich soil along streams or on slopes with a northern or eastern exposure.

TULIP TREE (*Liriodendron tulipfera*)

Like the white ash, this tree is valued for its wood, which is lightweight and relatively soft—once a popular canoe material but now used for general construction, furniture, plywood, insulation, crating, and fine book paper. It is sold commercially as yellow poplar, although it is not a poplar but a member of the magnolia family. (The only other tulip tree in the world grows in China and Vietnam.) It is a tall, straight tree that can attain the height of 200 feet, especially in the rich soil of Appalachian valleys, though it usu-

White Ash *(Fraxinus americana)* in mid-May (left) and in late September (right); see page 63.
John Bova

ally averages 150 feet. The tuliplike flowers that give the tree its name are orange at the base and greenish yellow on top, and they stand erect on the branchlets, making a glorious springtime display. The flowers produce a great deal of nectar, which attracts bees; the seeds are winged, dispersed by air, and provide food for many birds and small mammals. Larger animals, such as deer and rabbits, often browse on the bark and buds as well as on saplings, making this an important tree for wildlife. Found throughout the east, the tulip tree usually grows with other species, including white oak, beech, maple, white pine, and hemlock.

AMERICAN SYCAMORE (Platanus occidentalis)

Another large deciduous tree of the eastern woodlands is this fast-growing species that often exceeds one hundred feet in height. It grows in many different types of soil, even very wet areas, but is most often found along streams, where willows, maples, and cottonwoods are also common. Huge sycamores once lined the Ohio River, where John James Audubon described finding thousands of swallows living in a great hollow sycamore. The tree is easy to identify since its bark flakes off, revealing new green bark beneath, giving the tree a mottled appearance; it also has distinctive fruits, round, dry balls that hang on stalks, which give the tree its other common name, buttonwood. The wood is hard and difficult to split, though it is not very strong. It is used in making furniture and butcher blocks.

SHAGBARK HICKORY (Carya ovata)

Another lowland tree, but far better known, is this member of the hickory genus of the walnut family. With other hickories and the oaks, it is a major component of the eastern forest, and it is a valuable tree for many reasons. Its wood is heavy, tough, and especially resilient, making it useful for tool handles, furniture, and wagon wheels, but it is particularly prized as fuel, for it produces a great deal of heat for its volume and is slow-burning. It also gives a special flavor to meat and is frequently used for smoking hams.

Shagbark Hickory (Carya ovata)
Russ Kinne

Tulip Tree
(*Liriodendron tulipfera*; see page 63.)
John Serrao

Hickory nuts are sweet and rich and were a staple for Indians who ground them for baking. A tall tree, growing to 150 feet, the well-named shagbark hickory is easily identified by its bark, which breaks off in plates, attached to the tree in the middle but curling outward at the ends. Like all hickories, the shagbark produces large amounts of pollen in the spring and causes some humans to suffer hay fever; this pollen usually appears before the leaves are fully grown so that fertilization is more likely than it would be later in the season.

BLACK WALNUT (*Juglans nigra*)

Unfortunately for humans, the black walnut is a relatively slow-growing tree, and most of the giant specimens that once covered the east are now gone, due to this tree's enormous value for both its wood and its fruit. Nevertheless, the tree still flourishes, especially in low-lying areas, though it rarely reaches heights of over 100 feet, where once it grew to 150 or more. Years ago the black walnut, with its beautiful brown, grained wood, was used to make split-rail fences, houses, and furniture, but now its use is restricted to veneers rather than whole pieces. Because it does not warp and because it absorbs shock well, it has been an ideal wood for making rifle stocks. Although black walnuts are considered a delicacy, especially in the making of candy and ice cream, it is the English walnut, an imported species widely cultivated in North America, that produces the light-colored nuts sold commercially.

PECAN (*Carya illinoensis*)

Before we leave the walnut family, let's take a look at this other valuable nut-producing tree, which once grew primarily in the Mississippi River valley, preferring rich bottomland and humid climate, since its nuts take a long time to reach maturity. Now the tree is cultivated far beyond its original range, throughout the south, Georgia being the principal pecan grower today. The wood is used commercially, but the tree is valued mostly for its nuts; in fact, in the days when our forests were thought to be inexhaustible, settlers would cut down huge trees just for a single harvest of nuts, which in a large tree might be as much as one thousand pounds. The pecan is the tallest of the hickories, sometimes reaching two hundred feet, and they are long-lived, producing nuts as long as two hundred years. Thomas Jefferson once sent George Washington some pecan nuts, then called "Illinois nuts," and they were planted at Mount Vernon in 1786 where the trees still survive.

Ohio Buckeye (*Aesculus glabra*; see page 72.)
Richard Parker

Black Walnut (*Juglans nigra*)
Tom McHugh

Pecan
(Carya illinoensis; see page 68.)
Larry Nicholson

OHIO BUCKEYE *(Aesculus glabra)*

This medium-size tree, which averages fifty feet in height, is commonly found growing with other species, in both maple-beech forests and in oak-hickory stands. Its range is relatively restricted from the Alleghenies to central Texas, and it is becoming increasingly rare as these forests are cut down to accommodate human habitations. The wood is light and easy to carve, so it has found many uses, but is not widely used commercially because of its scarcity. Like the horsechestnut, which is also in the buckeye family, this tree produces a chestnutlike seed, but buckeye nuts are to be avoided as they are not edible. This species also produces a foul-smelling odor when its leaves, bark, or twigs are crushed, giving it the nickname "fetid buckeye." Nevertheless, Ohio chose to make it the state tree, calling itself the Buckeye State.

BLACK WILLOW *(Salix nigra)*

Although this species ranges widely throughout the east, it grows best in the Mississippi River valley where it is often found in pure stands in wet areas along streams and in swamps. Like all willows, it has a bulky root system that makes it a valuable tree for preventing soil erosion, reinforcing banks of rivers in floods and being used to build dams. Although the tree may reach a height of sixty feet or more, making this our largest willow, the trunk is not straight but forked with sweeping branches. Trees in the northern part of the range tend to be much smaller than those in the south. The leaves are long and the branchlet wood is light and springy, making it useful for basketry and furniture. Wild animals often feed on new branches and use the trees for cover. There are perhaps eighty species of willow in North America, some of them capable of surviving in the tundra regions where no other trees will grow. One of our most familiar willows, the weeping willow, is not a native tree but was introduced from China early in the eighteenth century.

Black Tupelo *(Nyssa sylvatica;* see page 74.)
Dr. Wm. M. Harlow

Black Willow *(Salix nigra)*
Edmund Appel

72

Flowering Dogwood
(*Cornus florida*)
Leonard Lee Rue III

BLACK TUPELO (*Nyssa sylvatica*)

This is another species that grows in low-lying areas, although it can adapt to upland ground unlike most other tupelos, which prefer swampy areas. It is a lovely tree, often exceeding one hundred feet in height, with a straight trunk and rounded crown of leaves that are brilliantly colored in autumn. The greenish flowers, which bloom in spring, attract bees with their nectar, and the fruit—a blue bitter-tasting berry—is a favorite of many wild animals. Although the wood is sometimes used to build docks, the tree is valued by humans mostly for its ornamental use.

FLOWERING DOGWOOD (*Cornus florida*)

There are about forty dogwood species in North America,
but this is perhaps the best known, for it grows from Massachusetts south to Florida and west to Texas, often near or under many tall trees, such as oaks, hickories, tulip trees, beeches, maples, and pines. Now known primarily as an ornamental tree, prized for its beautiful flowers, the dogwood is also valuable for its wood, which is tough and close-grained; once it was used in great quantity by the weaving industry which found it ideal as a material for making shuttles, but now it is employed for tool handles, golf clubs, and occasionally jewelers' blocks. The flowers are actually tiny and inconspicuous, growing in clusters within showy white or pink bracts, or leaves. They bloom in spring before the leaves appear, eventually producing bright red berries, toxic to humans but eaten by many birds and small mammals. The tree may grow as high as fifty feet but is often

Black Haw
(*Viburnum prunifolium*)
A. W. Ambler

smaller, making up the understory of the forest, like the hawthorns and hornbeams.

BLACKHAW (*Viburnum prunifolium*)

This is another small tree valued primarily for its lovely flowers. Growing along the edge of the forest, in clearings, or on hillsides, the blackhaw rarely grows higher than thirty feet and it branches closely to the ground so that it looks like a large bush. The flowers are clustered white blossoms, which produce dark blue berrylike fruits in fall, a favorite food of many birds and rodents. Because the tree is so small, it is of little commercial importance as a timber source, but is planted as an ornamental, as is its close relative the nannyberry (*Viburnum lentago*).

EASTERN RED CEDAR (*Juniperus virginiana*)

Up to now, we have met only deciduous trees in this varied eastern hardwood forest, but there are a number of coniferous trees in the area, the most widespread one being this species, a member of the cypress family and not a true cedar. It can be found growing in swamp areas and on rocky hillsides, but is most commonly seen in old fields and along with hickories and oaks in open woods. A slow-growing tree that can live up to four hundred years, the red cedar produces blue berrylike fruits that are an important food for several species of birds. The wood is light and brittle but easily carved and was once the primary material for pencils. Cedar oil effectively repels moths, though it is used as a perfume for humans, and so the wood was commonly used as a lining for closets and chests.

White Pine
(Pinus strobus)
A. W. Ambler

PITCH PINE (Pinus rigida)

Unlike the white pine, which is in the soft-pine group, the pitch pine is a hard pine, with close-grained wood and a hard spiny cone. It, too, ranges widely throughout the northeast, often in low-lying areas. Because it can grow in poor soil, the pitch pine is often used in reestablishing forest; it can also survive forest fires, since its cones, which can remain unopened for years, will deposit their seeds after a fire. The wood is weak but resistant to decay and has been used in construction and to manufacture turpentine. Although the tree is often found growing with other trees, such as white pine, oaks, and birches, it is the dominant tree in one particularly interesting place, the pine barrens of New Jersey. In this large area of over a million acres exists a coniferous forest very unlike that farther north; because the soil is so poor, the trees are stunted and twisted, with long roots that absorb water deep in the earth and anchor the trees so that they are able to withstand hurricanes. Mosses, lichens, and hardy bushes grow there, along with curious carnivorous plants, such as the sundew and pitcher plant, which trap insects as food because there is so little of nutritional value in the earth.

WHITE PINE (Pinus strobus)

This extremely important member of the pine family is widely distributed throughout the northeast, usually found with white ash, eastern hemlock, as well as other species. Vast stands of white pine once covered the area, and early settlers quickly discovered the high quality of the wood— light, strong, with a tendency to have less resin and to warp less than other pines—which has made it a valuable timber species. It was ideal as a source of masts for sailing ships, since the trees can grow over two hundred feet in height. Although the virgin forests are now gone, the tree is, fortunately, rather fast-growing and the third growth has reached maturity, so that it is still important commercially. The tree is also used as an ornamental, for it can be easily shaped by pruning, and is often seen as landscaping along highways and in parks and backyards.

Eastern Red Cedar (Juniperus virginiana)
Michael P. Gadomski

Pitch Pine
(*Pinus rigida*; see page 77.)
Miriam Reinhart

EASTERN HEMLOCK *(Tsuga canadensis)*

There are four North American species of hemlock, two in the west and two in the east. They are an ancient group, and fossils of leaves and cones have been found in North America indicating that they existed here many millennia ago. The eastern hemlock is relatively large, sometimes over 150 feet tall, and it prefers shaded, protected areas, such as eastern slopes and valleys. Although a tree may be forty years old before it begins to produce seeds, some hemlocks live nearly one thousand years. Humans have found little use for the wood, which is weak and coarsely grained and unsuitable for lumber; it is also limited as a fuel wood since it sends out sparks. The bark, however, contains tannin, which has been used to heal wounds and tan leather. Wild animals find the tree very useful since it provides shelter and is a source of food. The seeds are tiny and though they are produced in great quantity only a few of them will become trees.

Eastern Hemlock
(Tsuga canadensis)
William J. Jahoda

TREES OF THE SOUTHEAST

Longleaf Pine
(*Pinus palustris*)
Dr. Wm. M. Harlow

Along the Atlantic coast south of New York and extending into Florida and around the Gulf to Texas lies a coastal plain, the northern tip of which we met in the last chapter with the pitch pine. Because this area is relatively recent, geologically speaking, it is not rich in humus-laden earth like areas farther north and west, nor does it have mountainous regions to provide protected slopes. Nevertheless, trees are common here, with pines in the poor-soil areas, deciduous trees in the wetter sites, and a variety of fascinating species in the subtropical parts of Florida, where the warm climate and swampy land are host to a number of immigrants from the Caribbean islands.

LONGLEAF PINE (*Pinus palustris*)

Along with loblolly and slash pines, this species is charac-

Live Oak (*Quercus virginiana*)
Tomas D. W. Friedmann

teristic of the southeast, growing in poor soil but managing to achieve a height of over one hundred feet. Its trunk is straight, making it a valuable source for lumber as well as turpentine and tar. Squirrels and birds find cover in its branches and feed on its seeds which develop in long, cylindrical cones. The longleaf pine is so named because its needles can be as long as eighteen inches, growing in bundles that give the tree a graceful appearance. Although slow-growing, this tree can live as long as three hundred years.

LIVE OAK (*Quercus virginiana*)

Just as pine forests are considered a characteristic southern landscape, so is this tree, draped as it often is with Spanish moss, an epiphytic plant that gets its nutrients from the air and from rainfall rather than from the earth. Live oaks are usually found growing with other deciduous trees, including magnolias, holly, sweetgum, and other southern species of

oak. It is distinctive in appearance because of its wide-spreading crown and thick trunk. The flowers grow in catkins and the acorns, which are edible and an important food source to many species of wildlife, are elongated; unlike many other oaks, however, the leaves remain green and are not deeply lobed. The wood is durable and strong and is used for construction, though it is perhaps more valuable as firewood, since the wood is exceptionally heavy and dense.

CABBAGE PALMETTO (Sabal palmetto)

This slender tree is found along the coastal plain and throughout Florida where it is the state tree. Some palmettos are shrubs, planted ornamentally in many areas, but this species can grow as high as eighty feet, making it ideal for cultivation along roads and broad avenues. The tree grows naturally in marshes or in sandy soil along the coast, where it can thrive in full sun or in shade. Its leaves are large and fan-shaped with long blades (up to six feet). In the spring, the tree produces large hanging clusters of white flowers, which eventually become globe-shaped dry fruits that contain one seed each.

SOUTHERN CATALPA (Catalpa bignonioides)

This tree is another popular street tree, since it is a fast-growing species with a straight trunk and rounded crown that produces beautiful white flowers in the spring. It originally grew inland of the coastal plain, primarily in Louisiana, where it favors streambanks and rich, moist soil, but it has been cultivated far beyond its range, into southern New England and west to Texas. The fruit, which is a pod containing many flat seeds tufted with white hair, is not eaten much by wildlife, and the wood is of little commercial value to humans, but the showy flowers, which appear in early summer, make it an attractive ornamental.

Cabbage Palmetto (Sabal palmetto)
Kenneth W. Fink

Southern Catalpa
(Catalpa bignonioides)
Russ Kinne

Bald Cypress
(*Taxodium distichum*)
Sam C. Pierson, Jr.

Southern Magnolia
(*Magnolia grandiflora*)
Russ Kinne

SOUTHERN MAGNOLIA (*Magnolia grandiflora*)

This beautiful flowering tree symbolizes the south to many people. Although many species in the magnolia family, which is a very ancient and primitive group, are shrubs, this one is a large tree, reaching one hundred feet or more in height, especially in rich, moist soil, although it also grows in swamps and on low hills. The wood is hard but because it turns brown after exposure to air, it is of limited commercial value except as an ornamental tree. The flowers are large and white, with many long petals, and they are fragrant; the fruits look like cones, containing bright red seeds that are eaten by some birds and mammals. The leaves are large, dark, and shiny, remaining green year-round.

BALD CYPRESS (*Taxodium distichum*)

This coniferous tree also likes damp soil and is usually found along streams and in swamps of the southeast. It often grows in pure stands and in very wet areas its roots will protrude from the earth, looking like knees that help support the trunk. Wetlands are rich in animal life—from insects to birds and a number of mammals—and the bald cypress provides cover and food in the form of seeds, bark, and roots, as well as saplings. The bald cypress can live five hundred years or more, but because of its value as a timber tree, its wood being resistant to decay and easy to work, and because so much swampland has been drained in recent years, the tree is becoming increasingly rare except in parks and preserves. It is an attractive tree, sometimes reaching 120 feet in height, is often grown ornamentally, and has been cultivated far north of its range, even in dry upland locations.

FLORIDA STRANGLER FIG (*Ficus aurea*)

This curious member of the mulberry family is related to many valuable species, including mulberries, figs, breadfruit, and marijuana, but it is of little value to humans ei-

Florida Strangler Fig (*Ficus aurea*)
J. H. Robinson

FLORIDA ROYAL PALM (*Roystonea elata*)

Like the strangler fig, this tree is native to the southern part of Florida and is a member of a tree family that is most common in tropical and subtropical parts of the world. The coconut palm is unquestionably the most familiar palm tree, but it is not native to Florida, having been imported from Asia many years ago. The royal palm is tall, over one hundred feet, and has a straight unbranched trunk with a bright green crown of long leaves, some as long as thirteen feet. The flowers, which appear in spring in dense white clusters, are fragrant, and the fruits are round and smooth, turning black at maturity in late summer. As the name indicates, they are regal in appearance and are often planted along streets or around buildings to create a formal look. Unlike the coconut or date palm, both grown commercially in many areas for their fruit, the royal palm is valued solely for its handsome appearance.

Although we have looked at only a fraction of the large number of tree species that exist in North America, it is not difficult to appreciate the immense variety and value of these noble members of the plant kingdom. The mysterious beauty of the northern forests, the dramatic landscapes of our western mountain ranges, the picturesque nature of the Monterey coast or the Arizona desert, the colorful quality of the deciduous woodlands with their spring flowers and autumn foliage, and the intriguing lifeforms in subtropical Florida—all of this combines to shape our view of America. Imagine the wonderment of the early settlers at the sight of vast forests that promised an endless supply of wood for their new civilization. Much of that original promise is gone now, along with the great chestnuts, elms, and sycamores, and many new species have appeared to serve human purposes, greatly changing the natural landscape. But in some wilderness areas, we may see North America as it has been for thousands of years, a precious heritage that we must all endeavor to preserve.

ther for its wood, which is weak and coarse-grained, or its fruit, though birds feed on it. Many trees, especially the cabbage palmetto, could even consider the tree an enemy, for it kills them—as its name implies—by wrapping its aerial roots around them, eventually depriving them of sun with its leaves. The tree produces flowers year-round, and its seeds are spread by the birds who eat the fruit. Because the seeds are sticky, they will lodge in the branches of its victim, sending roots down to the earth. As the roots enlarge and form the trunk of the tree, the strangler fig continues to spread until it not only kills its host but also covers a large area.

Florida Royal Palm
(*Roystonea elata*)
R. C. Hermes

STATE TREES

Alabama	Southern Longleaf Pine	Montana	Ponderosa Pine
Alaska	Sitka Spruce	Nebraska	Cottonwood
Arizona	Paloverde	Nevada	Singleleaf Pinyon
Arkansas	Pine	New Hampshire	White Birch
California	California Redwood	New Jersey	Red Oak
Colorado	Colorado Blue Spruce	New Mexico	Pinyon
Connecticut	White Oak	New York	Sugar Maple
Delaware	American Holly	North Carolina	Pine
District of Columbia	Scarlet Oak	North Dakota	American Elm
Florida	Sabal Palmetto	Ohio	Ohio Buckeye
Georgia	Live Oak	Oklahoma	Redbud
Hawaii	Candlenut	Oregon	Douglas Fir
Idaho	White Pine	Pennsylvania	Hemlock
Illinois	White Oak	Rhode Island	Red Maple
Indiana	Tulip Tree	South Carolina	Palmetto
Iowa	Oak	South Dakota	Black Hills Spruce
Kansas	Cottonwood	Tennessee	Tulip Tree
Kentucky	Kentucky Coffee Tree	Texas	Pecan
Louisiana	Cypress	Utah	Blue Spruce
Maine	Eastern White Pine	Vermont	Sugar Maple
Maryland	White Oak	Virginia	Dogwood
Massachusetts	American Elm	Washington	Western Hemlock
Michigan	White Pine	West Virginia	Sugar Maple
Minnesota	Red Pine	Wisconsin	Sugar Maple
Mississippi	Magnolia	Wyoming	Cottonwood
Missouri	Dogwood		

SUGGESTED READING

Readers who would like to become more familiar with tree species in North America may consult a number of excellent field guides.

The Audubon Society Field Guide to North American Trees, published by Alfred A. Knopf, Inc., is available in two editions, one devoted to trees of the eastern region and one to trees of the west. In addition to comprehensive descriptions of species in each area, the books are illustrated with full-color photographs.

The Golden Press edition of *Trees of North America: A Guide to Field Identification* by C. Frank Brockman is less comprehensive but includes nearly six hundred species and full-color drawings of details as well as whole trees and useful maps showing the range of each tree.

The Complete Trees of North America: Field Guide and Natural History by Thomas S. Elias, published by Van Nostrand Reinhold, contains general information about trees and very full descriptions of each of more than 750 species. Over two thousand illustrations are included, with range maps, details of leaves, fruit, and flowers, and special key guides to different types of trees.

INDEX OF TREES

Page numbers in **boldface** refer
to illustrations.

acacia, 54
alder, 27
alder, red (*Alnus rubra*), **20,** 411–46,
   44
apple, 21
arborvitae, 28, 31, 40
ash, prickly, **22**
ash, white (*Fraxinus americana*), 63,
   64, 77
aspen, quaking (*Populus tremuloides*),
   27, 32, **32,** 44

bayberry tree, 21
beech, 13, 59, 60, 63, 66, 72, 74
beech, American (*Fagus grandifolia*),
   59, 60, 63
beech, European, 60
birch, 13, 25, 27, 44, 61, 77

birch, European white, 32
birch, paper (*Betula papyrifera*), **13,** 25,
   27, 32
blackhaw (*Viburnum prunifolium*), 75,
   75
buckeye, Ohio (*Aesculus glabra*), **23,**
   68, 72

cactus, 51–54
cactus, saguaro (*Cereus giganteus*), **25,**
   51–54, **51**
catalpa, southern (*Catalpa bignonioides*), 84, **85**
cedar, eastern white (*Thuja
   occidentalis*), **28,** 31–32
cedar, incense, 28
cedar, white, 28
chestnut, 60
chestnut, American (*Castanea dendata*), 60, **60**
chestnut, great, 88

coniferous trees, 12, 15, 16, 21, 25,
   27–32, 43, 44, 57, 59, 75–80, 83,
   87
cottonwood, 44, 46, 66
cottonwood, black (*Populus trichocarpa*), **43,** 44
cottonwood, eastern, 24
cypress, 28, 31, 40, 49, 75–77
cypress, bald (*Taxodium distichum*), 28,
   40, **86,** 87
cypress, Monterey (*Cupressus macrocarpa*), 49, **49**

deciduous trees, 12, 15, 27, 44, 46,
   57–75, 83
dogwood, 16, 74–75
dogwood, flowering (*Cornus florida*),
   74–75, **74**

elm, 21, 88

elm, American (*Ulmus americana*), 13, 61, **61**
elm, slippery (*Ulma rubra*), 61

fig, Florida strangler (*Ficus aurea*), 87–88, **88**
fir, 27, 28, 40, 44
fir, balsam (*Abies balsamea*), 29, **29**
fir, big-cone Douglas, 44
fir, Douglas (*Pseudotsuga menziesii*), **18**, 28, 43–44, **43**
fir, red, 40
fir, white (*Abies concolor*), **46**, 48
forsythia, 13
fruit trees, 16

gardenia, 63
gingko, **14**, 28

hardwoods, 57
hawthorn, 75
hemlock, 28, 43, 44, 59, 66, 80
hemlock, eastern (*Tsuga canadensis*), **15**, 77, 80, **80**
hickory, 12, 21, 59, 63, 66–68, 72, 75, 79
hickory, shagbark (*Carya ovata*), 13–14, 66–68, **66**
holly, 83
hornbeam, 75
hornbeam, America, **12**, 61
hornbeam, American hop (*Ostrya virginiana*), 61, **62**
horsechestnut, 60, 72

Joshua tree (*Yucca brevifolia*), **53**, 54
juniper, 15, 28
juniper, Rocky Mountain (*Juniperus scopulorum*), **18**, **37**, 40

larch, 28, 31
legume, 54
lily, 54
loblolly, 83

magnolia, 63, 83, 87
magnolia, southern (*Magnolia grandiflora*), 87, **87**
maple, 12, 15, 21, 59, 63, 66, 72, 74
maple, red, 59
maple, silver, 59

maple, sugar (*Acer saccharum*), **57**, 59, 60
mesquite (*Prosopis velutina*), **51**, 54
mulberry, 87
mulberry, red, **22**

nannyberry (*Viburnum lentago*), 75

oak, 12, 21, 40, 59, 60, 62–63, 66, 72, 74, 75, 77, 83–84
oak, black, 13, 63
oak, interior live (*Quercus wislizenii*), 46, 48
oak, live (*Quercus virginiana*), **11**, 46, 83–84, **83**
oak, northern red, **16**, **23**
oak, red, 62
oak, white (*Quercus alba*), **62–63**, **63**, 66
olive, 63

palm, 15, 54
palm, coconut, 88
palm, date, 88
palm, Florida royal (*Roystonea elata*), 88, **89**
palmetto, cabbage (*Sabal palmetto*), **16**, 84, **84**, 88
pecan (*Carya illinoensis*), 68, **70**
pine, 15, 27, 28, 37–40, 59, 74, 83
pine, Great Basin bristecone, 13
pine, Jeffrey (*Pinus jeffreyi*), **38**, 40
pine, longleaf (*Pinus palustris*), **15**, 83, **83**
pine, Monterey (*Pinus radiata*), 13, **46**, 48–49
pine, pinyon (*Pinus edulis*), 37–40, **40**
pine, pitch (*Pinus rigida*), **19**, **78**, 77, 83
pine, ponderosa (*Pinus ponderosa*), **36**, 37, 40
pine, slash, 83
pine, sugar, 40
pine, white (*Pinus strobus*), 66, **76**, 77
plum, American, **21**
poplar, 44

red cedar, eastern (*Juniperus virginiana*), 75–77, **77**
redwood, 43, 46

redwood, coastal (*Sequoia sempervivens*), **14**, 40, **45**, 46
rhododendron, 12

sequoia, 13, 28
sequoia, giant (*Sequoiadendron giganteum*), 12, 28, **35**, 40, 46
Spanish moss, 83
spruce, 27, 28–29, 35–37, 43, 44
spruce, black, 29
spruce, Engelmann (*Picea engelmanni*), 35–37, **35**
spruce, Norway, 28
spruce, red, 29
spruce, white (*Picea glauca*), **27**, 28–29
sumac, shining, **17**
sweetgum, 24, 83
sycamore, 88
sycamore, American (*Platanus occidentalis*), **57**, 66

tamarack (*Larix laricina*), 31, **31**, 32
taxodium, 28, 40
torreya, 28
tulip tree (*Liriodendron tulipfera*), 63–66, **67**, 74
tupelo, black (*Nyssa sylvatica*), **72**, 74

walnut, 66–68
walnut, black (*Juglans nigra*), 68, **68**
walnut, English, 68
Washingtonia, California (*Washingtonia filifera*), 54, **55**
willow, 12, 27, 44, 63, 66, 72
willow, black (*Salix nigra*), 72, **72**
willow, weeping, 72

yew, 12, 28, 44
yew, Pacific, **19**
yucca, 54